A TRUE BOOK™

My United States

Oregon

JOSH GREGORY

Children's Press®
An Imprint of Scholastic Inc.

Content Consultant
James Wolfinger, PhD, Associate Dean and Professor
College of Education, DePaul University, Chicago, Illinois

Library of Congress Cataloging-in-Publication Data
Names: Gregory, Josh, author.
Title: Oregon / by Josh Gregory.
Description: New York, NY : Children's Press, an imprint of Scholastic Inc., 2018. | Series: A true book | Includes
    bibliographical references and index.
Identifiers: LCCN 2017048740 | ISBN 9780531235751 (library binding) | ISBN 9780531250884 (pbk.)
Subjects: LCSH: Oregon—Juvenile literature.
Classification: LCC F876.3 .G74 2018 | DDC 979.5—dc23
LC record available at https://lccn.loc.gov/2017048740

Photographs ©: cover: Richard Hallman/Aurora Photos; back cover bottom: TayHam Photography/Shutterstock; back cover ribbon:
AliceLiddelle/Getty Images; 3 bottom: Gennaro Caninchello/Alamy Images; 3 top: Jim McMahon/Mapman ®; 4 top: Tim UR/Shutterstock;
4 bottom: Musat/iStockphoto; 5 bottom: Randy Shropshire/Getty Images; 5 top: Dennis Frates/Alamy Images; 7 top: steve bly/Alamy
Images; 7 center bottom: Kirkendall-Spring Photographers/Minden Pictures; 7 center top: All Canada Photos/Alamy Images; 7 bottom:
thinair28/Getty Images; 8-9: Steve Terrill/Getty Images; 11: Witold Skrypczak/Getty Images; 12: David Hanson/Aurora Photos; 13: Michael
Heiman/Getty Images; 14: Dennis Frates/Alamy Images; 15: Donald E. Hall/Getty Images; 16-17: 4kodiak/iStockphoto; 19: Portland Police
Bureau/AP Images; 20: Tigatelu/Dreamstime; 22 left: Atlaspix/Shutterstock; 22 right: Stockbyte/Getty Images; 23 bottom left: Musat/
iStockphoto; 23 top left: Cube/Ikon Images/Superstock, Inc.; 23 top right: David Brownell/Alamy Images; 23 bottom right: Radius/
Superstock, Inc.; 23 center right: Tim UR/Shutterstock; 23 center left: mikeledray/Shutterstock; 24-25: Universal History Archive/Getty
Images; 27: Library of Congress/Getty Images; 29: The Granger Collection; 30 bottom right: Universal History Archive/Getty Images; 30 top:
The Granger Collection; 30 bottom left: Library of Congress/Getty Images; 31 bottom left: Fotosearch/Getty Images; 31 top right: JerryPDX/
Getty Images; 31 bottom right: Tristan Fortsch/KATU-TV/AP Images; 31 top left: Atlaspix/Shutterstock; 32: Greg Vaughn/Alamy Images; 33:
nsf/Alamy Images; 34-35: Png-Studio/Getty Images; 36: Jonathan Ferrey/Getty Images; 37: andipantz/Getty Images; 38: Steve Terrill/Getty
Images; 39: Cultura Limited/Superstock, Inc.; 39 inset: Fuzzbass/Getty Images; 40 inset: Aleksandrov Ilia/Shutterstock; 40 background:
PepitoPhotos/Getty Images; 41: Gaertner/Alamy Images; 42 top left: IanDagnall Computing/Alamy Images; 42 top right: Terry Smith/Getty
Images; 42 bottom left: Dan Tuffs/Getty Images; 42 bottom right: Bloomberg/Getty Images; 43 top left: Paul Redmond/Getty Images; 43
top right: Agence Opale/Alamy Images; 43 bottom center: Aaron M. Sprecher/CHERA/AP Images; 43 center left: JB Lacroix/Getty Images;
43 bottom left: imageBROKER/Alamy Images; 43 bottom right: Randy Shropshire/Getty Images; 44 bottom left: Craig Dietrich/Flickr; 44
top left: Ethan Miller/Getty Images; 44 bottom right: Peter Dazeley/Getty Images; 44 top right: Andrii Gorulko/Alamy Images; 45 top right:
Robert Glusic/Getty Images; 45 top left: Mitch Diamond/Getty Images; 45 bottom left: picturelibrary/Alamy Images; 45 bottom right:
mikeledray/Shutterstock.

Maps by Map Hero, Inc.

Scholastic Inc., 557 Broadway, New York, NY 10012

1 2 3 4 5 6 7 8 9 10 R 28 27 26 25 24 23 22 21 20 19

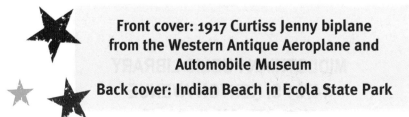

**Front cover: 1917 Curtiss Jenny biplane
from the Western Antique Aeroplane and
Automobile Museum**
Back cover: Indian Beach in Ecola State Park

Welcome to Oregon

Find the Truth!

Everything you are about to read is true *except* for one of the sentences on this page.

Which one is **TRUE**?

T or F Oregon grows more Christmas trees than any other state.

T or F Many people traveled to Oregon along the Oregon Trail during the 1700s.

UNITED STATES

Oregon

Find the answers in this book.

3

Contents

THE BIG TRUTH!

Hazelnuts

What Represents Oregon?

Beaver

Silver Falls
State Park

Aminé

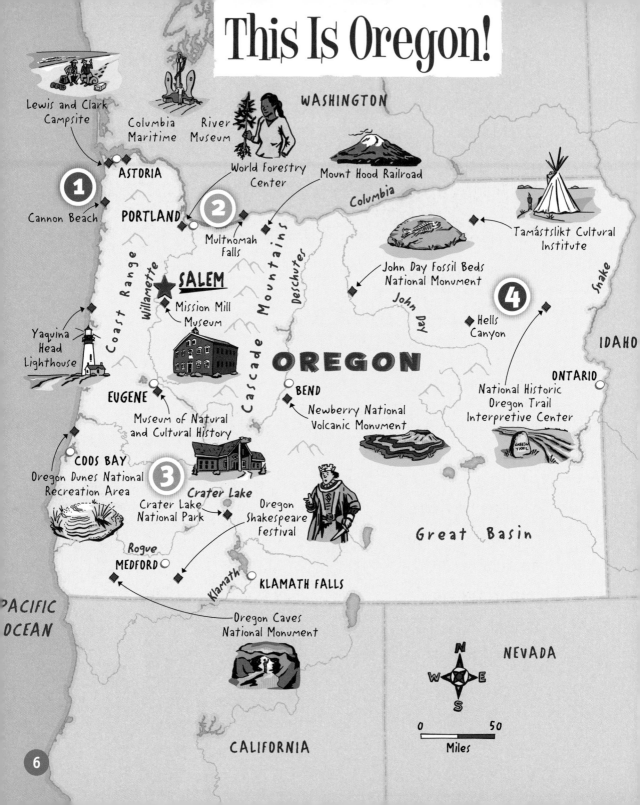

This Is Oregon!

Lewis and Clark Campsite

Columbia Maritime River Museum

WASHINGTON

World Forestry Center

Mount Hood Railroad

(1) ASTORIA

Cannon Beach

PORTLAND

(2)

Multnomah Falls

Columbia

Tamástslikt Cultural Institute

Coast Range

Willamette

SALEM
Mission Mill Museum

Cascade Mountains

Deschutes

John Day Fossil Beds National Monument

John Day

(4)

Snake

IDAHO

Yaquina Head Lighthouse

OREGON

Hells Canyon

ONTARIO

EUGENE

Museum of Natural and Cultural History

BEND

Newberry National Volcanic Monument

National Historic Oregon Trail Interpretive Center

COOS BAY

Oregon Dunes National Recreation Area

(3)

Crater Lake

Crater Lake National Park

Oregon Shakespeare Festival

Great Basin

Rogue

MEDFORD

Klamath

KLAMATH FALLS

Oregon Caves National Monument

PACIFIC OCEAN

NEVADA

N
W   E
S

CALIFORNIA

0   50
Miles

1 Cannon Beach

This Pacific Coast beach is a great place for sand and sun. It is also home to the towering Haystack Rock (pictured), a rock formation that rises 235 feet (72 meters) above the water's surface.

2 Multnomah Falls

Oregon is home to several tall waterfalls, but Multnomah Falls is the tallest of all. Its waters crash down to the ground from 620 feet (189 m) above.

3 Crater Lake National Park

The centerpiece of Oregon's only national park is an enormous lake in the **caldera** of an ancient volcano. At 2,000 feet (610 m) deep, it is the country's deepest lake.

IDAHO

4 Hells Canyon

Located in eastern Oregon, Hells Canyon is the country's deepest gorge. It measures nearly 8,000 feet (2,438 m) from top to bottom!

UTAH

With a height of 10,495 feet (3,199 m), Mount Jefferson is Oregon's second-highest peak after Mount Hood.

CHAPTER 1

Land and Wildlife

Located in the heart of the Pacific Northwest, Oregon is famous for its breathtaking natural scenery. It is home to snowy mountain peaks, dense green forests, and dry deserts. Rushing rivers and deep blue lakes are spread throughout the state. The rocky coastline and sandy beaches of the Pacific Ocean lie along the state's western edge. This wide range of outdoor environments makes Oregon a fascinating state.

Geography

The Pacific Coast forms Oregon's western border.
To the north is Washington State. The mighty
Columbia River forms most of the border between
these two states. One of the largest rivers in the
country, the Columbia flows 1,243 miles (2,000
kilometers) from Canada into the Pacific Ocean.
Idaho lies to Oregon's east, while California and
Nevada are to the south.

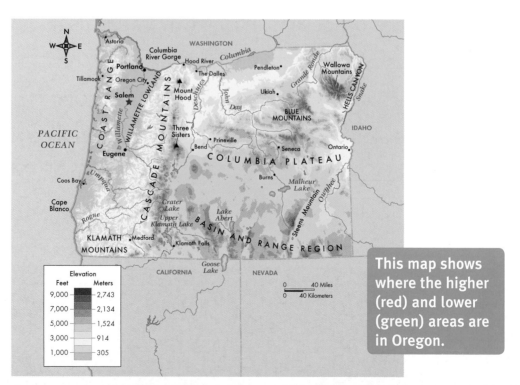

This map shows
where the higher
(red) and lower
(green) areas are
in Oregon.

Mount Hood

With a height of 11,239 feet (3,426 m), the **summit** of Mount Hood is the highest point in Oregon. This volcano was originally named Wy'east by the Multnomah people, who have lived in the area for hundreds of years. Its snowy slopes make it a popular destination in northwestern Oregon for skiers and snowboarders. Mount Hood is home to the only ski resort in the country where people can ski year-round. Climbers and hikers also enjoy the challenge of trying to reach the mountain's snowy highest points.

The western part of Oregon is filled with dense forests, **fertile** farmland, and river valleys. Heading east, about a third of the way across the state, the Cascade Mountains cut through from north to south. On the eastern side of the Cascades, the land takes on a different look. Sparse desert areas, wide-open grasslands, and dramatic rock formations are a common sight in eastern Oregon.

A man bikes across the wide-open, sandy landscape of southeastern Oregon.

MAXIMUM TEMPERATURE 119°F

MINIMUM TEMPERATURE -54°F

Light, drizzling rain is a common occurrence in Oregon's western towns and cities, such as Eugene.

Climate

Weather in Oregon is usually mild. This can, however, vary depending on the location and the time of year. West of the Cascades, the state sees a lot of rain. Some areas receive as much as 200 inches (508 centimeters) per year! During winters, weeks can pass without a single sunny day. Eastern Oregon tends to be drier. Some areas in the southeastern part of the state receive only about 15 inches (38 cm) of rain each year.

Western Oregon's wet, mild climate is perfect for growing dense, green forests. Here, moss grows on the spruce trees of Silver Falls State Park in the northwestern part of the state.

Plants

With its variety of environments and weather, Oregon is home to a diverse range of plants. In the west, forests of **conifers** such as pine trees and Douglas firs stretch as far as the eye can see. Enormous redwood trees can tower more than 350 feet (107 m) above the ground. In the east, short sagebrush plants dot the landscape. They thrive in the area's drier climate. Many colorful wildflower species also grow throughout Oregon.

Animals

Many wild animal species are native to Oregon, from black bears and enormous elk to raccoons and marmots. Seals, sea lions, and otters live along the Pacific coast. Farther out in the ocean waters, whales and dolphins can be seen surfacing for air. Throughout the state, majestic bald eagles soar through the sky in search of prey below. Salmon and trout swim through the rushing waters of Oregon's rivers and streams.

The Seal Rocks, a group of large rocks located along Oregon's coast, are named for the seals and sea lions that live in the area.

Oregon has had three capitols. The two previous buildings burned down.

CHAPTER **2**

Government

Salem, located in northwestern Oregon, has been the capital since Oregon became a state in 1859. Today, Salem is one of Oregon's largest cities and the center of activity for the state government. The current capitol has served the state since 1938. The building is topped with a 23-foot-tall (7 m) bronze statue of a pioneer. The statue represents the spirit of exploration and independence that led many settlers to the Oregon wilderness in the 1800s.

Three Branches

Like other states, Oregon has a government that is divided into three branches. The executive branch is led by the governor. It is responsible for carrying out state laws. The legislative branch, also called the Legislative Assembly, makes state laws. It consists of a 30-member senate and a 60-member house of representatives. The judicial branch is made up of Oregon's court system. It interprets the state's laws.

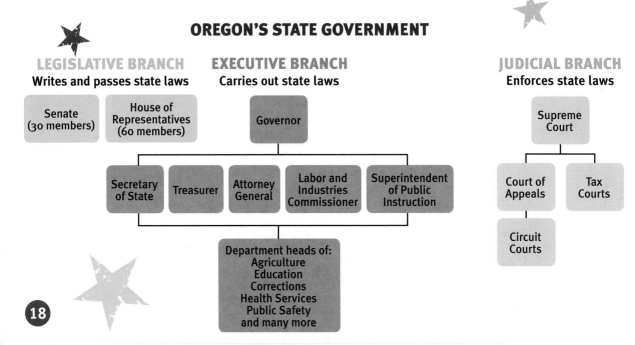

OREGON'S STATE GOVERNMENT

LEGISLATIVE BRANCH	EXECUTIVE BRANCH	JUDICIAL BRANCH
Writes and passes state laws	Carries out state laws	Enforces state laws

LEGISLATIVE BRANCH	EXECUTIVE BRANCH	JUDICIAL BRANCH
Senate (30 members) / House of Representatives (60 members)	Governor	Supreme Court
	Secretary of State / Treasurer / Attorney General / Labor and Industries Commissioner / Superintendent of Public Instruction	Court of Appeals / Tax Courts
	Department heads of: Agriculture Education Corrections Health Services Public Safety and many more	Circuit Courts

Local governments in Oregon oversee police and other important services. Here, Portland mayor Ted Wheeler shakes hands with the city's police chief, Danielle Outlaw.

Government by the People

Oregon's voters have a strong voice in their state's legislative process. In addition to electing officials to represent them in the state government, they vote directly on many new laws. They can also vote to undo any laws passed by the Legislative Assembly or to make changes to the state **constitution**. This process ensures that Oregon's government cannot pass laws that are widely unpopular with the state's people.

Oregon in the National Government

Each state elects officials to represent it in the U.S. Congress. Like every state, Oregon has two senators. The U.S. House of Representatives relies on a state's population to determine its numbers. Oregon has five representatives in the House.

Every four years, states vote on the next U.S. president. Each state is granted a number of electoral votes based on its number of members in Congress. With two senators and five representatives, Oregon has seven electoral votes.

2 senators and 5 representatives

7 electoral votes

With seven electoral votes, Oregon's voice in presidential elections is below average compared to other states.

The People of Oregon

Elected officials in Oregon represent a population with a range of interests, lifestyles, and backgrounds.

Ethnicity (2016 estimates)

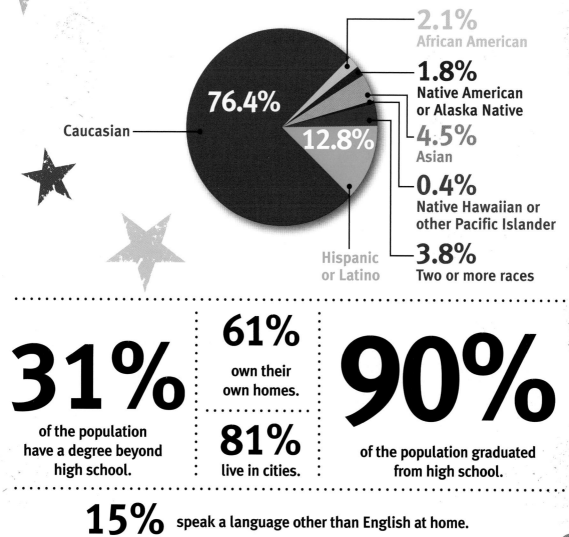

Caucasian — **76.4%**

12.8%
Hispanic or Latino

2.1%
African American

1.8%
Native American or Alaska Native

4.5%
Asian

0.4%
Native Hawaiian or other Pacific Islander

3.8%
Two or more races

31%
of the population have a degree beyond high school.

61%
own their own homes.

81%
live in cities.

90%
of the population graduated from high school.

15% speak a language other than English at home.

What Represents Oregon?

States choose specific animals, plants, and objects to represent the values and characteristics of the land and its people. Find out why these symbols were chosen to represent Oregon or discover surprising curiosities about them.

Seal

Oregon's state seal shows an eagle perched atop a shield. The shield displays several important symbols of Oregon and its history, including a covered wagon and the Pacific Coast.

Flag

Oregon's state flag has a different design on each side. One side displays the state seal. The other shows a beaver, one of Oregon's most important state symbols. Oregon is nicknamed the Beaver State.

Pear
STATE FRUIT
Pears are among the
many fruits that grow in
the orchards of Oregon's
Willamette River valley.

Oregon Swallowtail
STATE INSECT
This yellow and black butterfly
can be found in many parts of
the Pacific Northwest.

Hazelnut
STATE NUT
These nuts are also
known as filberts.

Douglas Fir
STATE TREE
These tall, green
conifers cover much
of western Oregon.

Milk
STATE BEVERAGE
Oregon is home to many
dairy farms, especially in the
northwestern part of the state.

Beaver
STATE ANIMAL
Beavers and their furs drew
many new residents to Oregon
in the state's early days.

Settlers making their way to the Pacific Northwest on the Oregon Trail often traveled together in large groups for safety.

CHAPTER 3

History

Oregon has long attracted new residents with its stunning beauty and proximity to valuable resources. These benefits encouraged early Native Americans to settle here. In the 1800s, farmers and frontiersmen rushed into the state. Even today, many people continue moving northwest. Each group to arrive has brought something new to the state, making it the incredible place it is today.

The First Settlers

People have lived in what is now Oregon for at least 13,000 years. The first people to arrive were hunters following mammoths and other huge prehistoric animals. Over time, these people settled down in Oregon. They built farms and villages and developed a variety of cultures. By the time Europeans started arriving in the late 1700s, Oregon's Native Americans spoke more than 20 languages. They also lived in dozens of different groups.

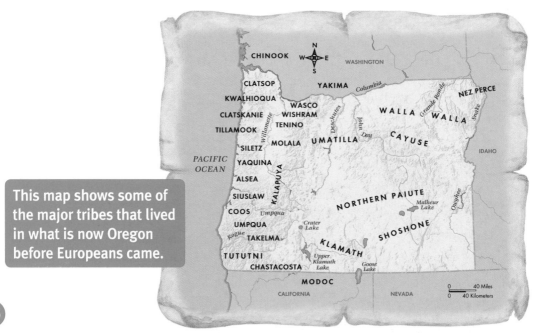

This map shows some of the major tribes that lived in what is now Oregon before Europeans came.

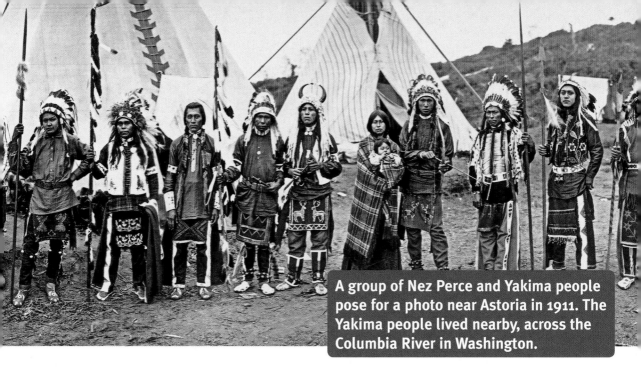

A group of Nez Perce and Yakima people pose for a photo near Astoria in 1911. The Yakima people lived nearby, across the Columbia River in Washington.

People who lived in northeastern Oregon, such as the Nez Perce, lived in villages some of the year. But they also traveled to hunting grounds for long stretches of time. In southeastern Oregon, where fewer plants grow, groups such as the Northern Paiute traveled more. They hunted small animals and gathered foods such as berries and seeds. Along the Pacific coast, the Clatsop, Tillamook, and other groups enjoyed rich farmland and plenty of fishing and hunting.

Europeans Arrive

In the 1500s, explorers from Spain and Great Britain sailed along the Pacific coast, but never set foot in Oregon. It was not until the late 1700s that Europeans started heading to the Pacific Northwest. The first Europeans to arrive came in search of valuable animal **pelts**. Some hunted the animals themselves, while others traded for them with Oregon's Native Americans. The Europeans then took the pelts back to the East Coast or shipped them overseas for sale.

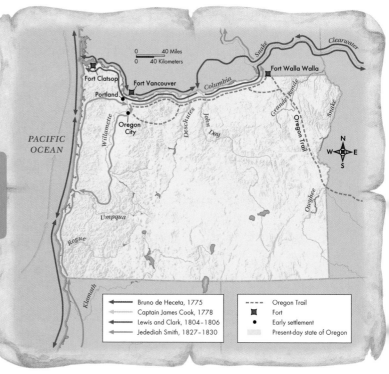

This map shows routes Europeans took as they explored and settled what is now Oregon.

Lewis and Clark relied on the help of a Shoshone woman named Sacagawea (left) as they explored the Pacific Northwest.

The Lewis and Clark Expedition

In 1803, U.S. president Thomas Jefferson purchased a huge portion of land from France. Called the Louisiana Purchase, this land spanned much of what is now the central United States. Jefferson sent Meriwether Lewis and William Clark to map the region and find a water route leading to the Pacific Ocean. The two men traveled across the Louisiana Purchase and into Oregon. They took notes about their route and the rich land they found in the Pacific Northwest. After they returned east, news of Oregon's potential spread.

Into the West

During the 1800s, many new settlers traveled to Oregon. Some people continued the tradition of fur trapping and trading in the region. Others came to take advantage of Oregon's excellent farmland. In the 1840s, thousands of farmers made the six-month journey from the Midwest to Oregon along the Oregon Trail. Many died as they traveled this long route in covered wagons.

Timeline of Oregon Events

11,000 BCE
Early people arrive in Oregon by this time.

1700s
Many Native American cultures thrive in Oregon.

1805
Lewis and Clark reach Oregon and settle down for the winter at Fort Clatsop.

1840s
Thousands of new settlers head to Oregon on the Oregon Trail.

| 11,000 BCE | 1700s | 1805 | 1840s |

From Territory to State

As Oregon's population grew, U.S. leaders began to see the importance of making the area an official part of the country. However, Great Britain also claimed much of the Pacific Northwest. After some negotiation, the border between American and British land was set, and the Oregon **Territory** was established in 1848. Finally, in 1859, Oregon became the country's 33rd state.

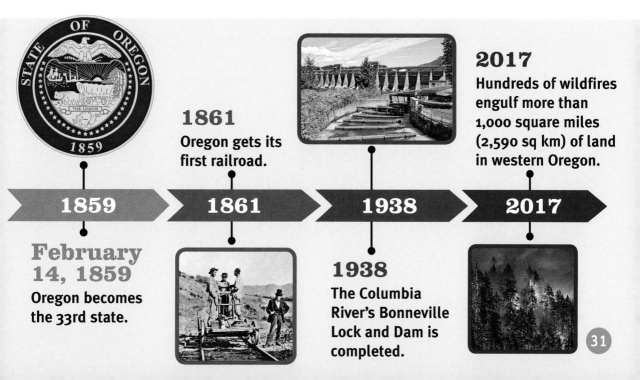

1861
Oregon gets its first railroad.

2017
Hundreds of wildfires engulf more than 1,000 square miles (2,590 sq km) of land in western Oregon.

1859 · **1861** · **1938** · **2017**

February 14, 1859
Oregon becomes the 33rd state.

1938
The Columbia River's Bonneville Lock and Dam is completed.

Many Native Americans still live on reservations today. Here, a rider attempts to stay on a bronco at a rodeo at central Oregon's Warm Springs Indian Reservation.

Growth and Change

As a state, Oregon became an important asset to the country. Throughout the 1800s and 1900s, it was a major source of **timber**, seafood, and other resources. But as Oregon's new residents prospered, Native Americans suffered. White settlers took over more land, while many of the state's Native Americans were forced onto **reservations**. Some Native Americans fought against this unfair treatment. Ultimately, however, they were pushed out of their homes.

Chief Joseph

Chief Joseph was born in northeastern Oregon's Wallowa Valley.

In 1877, a group of Oregon's Nez Perce resisted U.S. efforts to force them onto reservations. The resisters were led by Thunder Rolling Down the Mountain. Also known as Chief Joseph, he and his people fended off attacks from the U.S. Army while fleeing 1,400 miles (2,253 km) north toward Canada. Chief Joseph's 200 or so warriors won several battles against 2,000 U.S. Army troops. But by October 1877, the group was forced to surrender. The Nez Perce, however, are still celebrated for their brave struggle.

The Grand Floral Parade is one of the main events at the Portland Rose Festival, an annual celebration of the city's beautiful flowers.

CHAPTER 4

Culture

Today, Oregon is home to a diverse range of people. About half of them live in and around Portland. This city is a cultural center packed with museums, theaters, restaurants, and other fun places to go. Artists of all kinds, from painters and sculptors to writers and musicians, are drawn to Oregon for its laid-back attitude and inspiring scenery. All across the state, there are always new things to see and interesting people to meet.

Sports

Oregonians love to cheer for their local sports teams. The Portland Trail Blazers have been thrilling basketball fans for decades. The Portland Timbers soccer team has only been playing since 2011, but it has won a devoted audience.

College sports are also popular. The Oregon State University Beavers and University of Oregon Ducks have many passionate fans. The two schools are sports rivals, so it's a big deal in Oregon any time they face off.

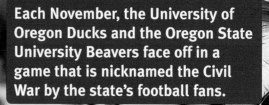

Each November, the University of Oregon Ducks and the Oregon State University Beavers face off in a game that is nicknamed the Civil War by the state's football fans.

Many neighborhoods in Portland regularly hold street festivals where people can enjoy live entertainment, food trucks, craft vendors, and more.

Celebrations

All year long, exciting events take place throughout Oregon. Every June for more than 100 years, the Portland Rose Festival has honored the roses that grow wild in parts of the state, including the city itself. There is a parade, concerts, and much more. In September, people flock to the small town of Pendleton. Here, they enjoy Oregon's biggest rodeo, the Pendleton Round-Up.

Oregon is one of the top states for cranberry farming. To harvest cranberries, farmers flood the area, then use special machines to shake the berries from the plants. The berries then float to the surface.

Oregon at Work

Oregonians make their living in a variety of industries. Many people still work in jobs related to agriculture, fishing, and timber. Tourism is also big business, as people come from all over the world to hike, climb, or simply enjoy the sights. Oregon is a center of the sportswear industry. Major companies such as Nike, Adidas, and Columbia Sportswear all have headquarters here.

When working with tiny, delicate electronics, workers often wear protective clothing to keep dust and hair from spreading.

Turning High-Tech

Oregon is becoming a major center of high-tech business. One of the biggest employers in the Portland area is Intel, a computer hardware manufacturer. Many of the state's newest companies are focused on computer software and Internet services. As a result, Oregon has turned into a hot spot for computer programmers and other tech experts.

Time to Eat!

With so many farms, there is no shortage of fresh, delicious food in Oregon. Freshly picked fruits and locally made cheese are found at farmers' markets around the state. In Portland, there are hundreds of food carts. These tiny, mobile restaurants serve everything from fast food to gourmet specialties.

★ Marionberry Crumble

Ask an adult to help you!

The marionberry is a variety of blackberry grown only in Oregon. If you can't find marionberries, you can use other kinds of blackberries.

Ingredients

$1/2$ cup butter, melted
2 cups flour
$1/4$ teaspoon salt
1 tablespoon baking powder

$1 \, 1/4$ cups milk
2 cups sugar, divided
5 cups marionberries

Directions

Preheat the oven to 350 degrees F. Pour the melted butter into a 9-by-13-inch baking pan. Mix the flour, salt, baking powder, milk, and 1 cup of the sugar in a bowl. Pour this mixture into the butter. Add the berries to the pan, then sprinkle the remaining 1 cup sugar over the top. Do not stir. Bake for $1 \, 1/2$ hours, or until brown and bubbly. Enjoy!

Sparks Lake and Broken Top Mountain are among the many beautiful natural landmarks of western Oregon.

An Incredible State

Oregon offers an awe-inspiring landscape unlike any other. Waves crash along the Pacific coast. Winds blow across the wide-open spaces in the east. This state is the perfect place to hike along a wooded mountainside or take a canoe trip down a river. It's also a great spot to relax on a beach or enjoy fine dining at a restaurant. Whether you live here or you're just passing through, Oregon is an amazing state to be in. ★

Famous People

Herbert Hoover

(1874–1964) was the 31st president of the United States. He lived in Newberg for several years in his youth.

Beverly Cleary

(1916–) is the best-selling author of the Ramona series and many other books for children and young adults. She was born in McMinnville.

Ursula K. Le Guin

(1929–2018) was the award-winning author of such novels as *The Left Hand of Darkness*, *The Dispossessed*, and the Earthsea series. She lived in Portland for most of her life.

Phil Knight

(1938–) is the founder of Nike and one of the most successful businesspeople in the world. He is from Portland.

Matt Groening

(1954–) is a cartoonist and animator best known for creating TV shows such as *The Simpsons* and *Futurama*. He is from Portland.

Jon Krakauer

(1954–) is an author who is famous for writing about real-life wilderness adventures. He is from Corvallis.

Kaitlin Olson

(1975–) is an actress and comedian who stars in the TV series *It's Always Sunny in Philadelphia* and *The Mick*. She grew up in the Portland area.

Aminé

(1994–) is a rapper who is best known for the hit song "Caroline." He is from Portland.

Esperanza Spalding

(1984–) is a Grammy Award–winning musician and songwriter. She was born and raised in Portland.

Ndamukong Suh

(1987–) is a pro football star who has played for the Detroit Lions and the Miami Dolphins. He was born and raised in Portland.

Did You Know That . . .

Nike, the world's largest athletic shoe company, was founded in Oregon. Its world headquarters is still located near Portland in the city of Beaverton.

Oregon is home to the world's smallest park. Mill Ends Park in Portland measures only about 2 feet (0.6 m) from one end to the other.

Almost all of the hazelnuts produced in the United States come from Oregon.

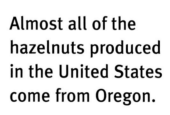

People are not allowed to pump their own gas in many parts of Oregon. Instead, gas station employees must operate the pumps.

Oregon has more ghost towns than any other state. Hundreds of abandoned settlements dot the state, and many are open to the public.

More Christmas trees are grown in Oregon than in any other state. The state produced more than five million holiday trees in 2016.

The Tillamook Cheese Factory, located along Oregon's coast, is one of the largest cheese factories in the world. It has been operating for more than 100 years.

Did you find the truth?

(T) Oregon grows more Christmas trees than any other state.

(F) Many people traveled to Oregon along the Oregon Trail during the 1700s.

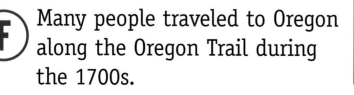

Resources

Books

Kent, Deborah. *Oregon*. New York: Children's Press, 2015.

Perritano, John. *The Lewis and Clark Expedition*. New York: Children's Press, 2010.

Rozett, Louise (ed.). *Fast Facts About the 50 States: Plus Puerto Rico and Washington, D.C.* New York: Children's Press, 2010.

Visit this Scholastic website for more information on Oregon:

★ www.factsfornow.scholastic.com
Enter the keyword **Oregon**

Important Words

caldera (kahl-DER-uh) a very large volcanic crater formed by the collapse of the central part of the volcano or by violent explosions

conifers (KAH-nif-urz) evergreen trees that produce their seeds in cones

constitution (kahn-stih-TOO-shuhn) the basic laws of a country or state that describe the rights of the people and the powers of the government

fertile (FUR-tuhl) good for growing crops and plants

pelts (PELTS) animal skins with the hair or fur still on them

reservations (rez-ur-VAY-shuhnz) areas of land set aside by the government for a special purpose, particularly land that belongs to Native American groups

summit (SUHM-it) the highest point

territory (TER-ih-tor-ee) a part of the United States that is not within any state but has its own legislature

timber (TIM-bur) cut wood used for building

Index

Page numbers in **bold** indicate illustrations.

About the Author

Josh Gregory is the author of more than 120 books for young readers. A former resident of Portland, Oregon, he currently lives in Chicago, Illinois.